I0236675

FOR MY LOVE ENDURES FOREVER

Poetry and Prose

BOOK 2

By

JOSEPH ANTHONY RUSSO

Order this book online at www.trafford.com
or email orders@trafford.com

Most Trafford titles are also available at major online book retailers.

© Copyright 2012 Joseph Anthony Russo.
All rights reserved. No part of this publication may be reproduced, stored in a retrieval system, or transmitted, in any form or by any means, electronic, mechanical, photocopying, recording, or otherwise, without the written prior permission of the author.

Printed in the United States of America.

ISBN: 978-1-4669-0531-3 (sc)
ISBN: 978-1-4669-0530-6 (hc)
ISBN: 978-1-4669-0532-0 (e)

Library of Congress Control Number: 2011960902

Trafford rev. 02/29/2012

Trafford PUBLISHING®   www.trafford.com

North America & International
toll-free: 1 888 232 4444 (USA & Canada)
phone: 250 383 6864 ♦ fax: 812 355 4082

Set me as a seal upon your heart,
as a seal upon your arm;
For love is as strong as death,
passion as fierce as the grave.
Its flashes are flames of fire,
a blazing flame.

Song of Solomon

Dedicated
to my wife,
Marjorie,
the reason for all
my enduring.

I write to keep open the ear and
eye of my heart, to strain to hear
your voice and see your face;
through the silence of God,
the distance between us,
and the nearness felt
within my heart.

Contents

Introduction

THE HISTORY

Another connotation for this book could be fire—an apt subject ever since Prometheus stole fire from Mount Olympus changing man's direction in life. Hearing the sound of my wife sighing my name for the last time signaled my change in direction. It was not unlike my sensing a spark of something indefinable that eventually grew from a flame into a roaring fire.

The world tells the grieving that death is their transition into a "new life;" the reverent say death is a manifestation of the will of God. My "new life" consisted of that which I knew with my wife and the continuation of life in which two have unexplainably now become one. And I carried with me all my fervent baggage about life, death, and the one I still love.

Although at the end there were emotions I needed to express to my wife, I didn't know what to say, how to begin, when to stop. I said nothing. And then it was too late to say anything. I did not understand if my wife had been abandoned by me or I had abandoned her, or even if God had abandoned both my wife and myself.

THE PROCESS

However, the import was not the actual words but in what they continue to speak of: The unquenchable fire of love consuming all who allow its burning to continue within their hearts. This may be called free choice. But for me there is nothing free about it, as it comes with the baggage alluded to. Also, there is no choice; there could be other way for me to continue in life. It's like a sort of dying to oneself to be reborn into a life of one from a life of two that was never extinguished.

Now feeling like a prisoner on earth and walking through a minefield of memories, I still felt the door to the one I love wasn't closed, unlike the world's view of life and death that the door was not only securely shut but also irrevocably locked, that love is imprisoned by the finality of death. The need to open that door caused me to feverishly write, child-like or not, churning out piece after piece, much in the way of a child scribbling on a sheet of paper, because I had become the child of a new reality. And like a child, the end results didn't matter as long as I felt my inspiration, my wife, was felt to be with me in this new reality.

In this way the spirit of my wife has never left me; we were not separated at the end of our journey on earth. It's as though we are only a room apart, writing letters to each other, to intimately share thoughts and emotions, seemingly to fall in love for the first time all over again. I am only trying to find the voice she would understand, the voice I needed and still need to express.

Statements that needed to have been said within the timeframe of life but which remain unsaid when death strikes remain within the safety of the heart. When the heart speaks, one cannot help but soulfully listen within the spiritual realm between life and death. And spiritual seems to be the right word—for what other would describe life when love is taken away but not removed from the heart? How else to explain the feelings of the heart felt more real than reality?

THE BOOKS

When completing the first book, I believed everything had been said that I could say. But its contents were only the initial flame. On these pages, as with Book 1, I have scribbled multifaceted self-portraits with my wife, my inspiration, as my center of interest, unabashedly sentimental in my attempts to express pathos, to put into words interior pain and anguish as metaphors of portraiture, and even confront the fear that paralyzes any life faced with a loss of identity, a best friend, a steadfast crutch in times of need. And there is yet more to say in the strains of the noble and sentimental waltz of Book 1 that never ends.

I remember the simple everyday tasks my wife and I once did for each other as we journeyed closely together through life, intrinsic and heartfelt memories that today still live within me. These will continue to grace the years we are apart in my hope that I served as a crutch for my wife during her years of greatest need, as my journey through life continues, always with the spirit of my wife, always with God, always by means of a fire within.

Joseph Anthony Russo

Mosaic design by Joseph Anthony Russo

FOR MY LOVE ENDURES FOREVER

PARTLY WHISPERED
Telling it as it is

I'm struggling to find the word I want to give you today,
Some people would just give up and go their own way,
That's most easy to do,
When there is nothing new,
But I'll search deep until I find what I need to say.
        (Let all the others give in,
          I'd find love on the head of a pin.)

It really wasn't so hard to for me to find the word love,
It really is the only word that fits you like a glove,
So in giving you this,
Bundled up with my kiss,
I'm telling the world that you're like no other above.
        (And I'm telling myself, too,
          That for me there is only you.) ♍

REMEMBRANCE SONG

Will you remember
the words of our song,
the euphony of my heart?
Silent today, always of love,
through time, the words we once spoke will dim,
but, yet, they all began at the sound of our hymn.

Will we remember
the truths from our past,
based on vows we once made?
Today they seem despairingly weak,
but time has quelled its ever-soulful mourning,
and you must know still of my hearts' burning.

I will remember
our footprints in life,
all those years we marked
side-by-side as we walked together,
the warm softness of your smile at a beginning,
the coldness of your silence heard in our ending.

But perhaps like Job
will you begin to bemoan
that happiness in life will not
be seen or lived by us ever again?
No. My heart still beats; its words still ring true;
our song is now my song: I will never forget you. ♍

At the beginning of our last day,
    you didn't move,
    your eyes closed,
    your lips slept,
fleeting time impartially flowed into our past.
I wish I knew what you were thinking.
Then I would unleash my fearful tongue.
Then I would pluck out my trembling heart.

But today all I have is your mystery,
like a rose with petals closed,
as if innocently asleep
lying upon a bed of stillness.
    All is silence here.
    All is muteness here.
As when you were here.
And I was with you. And I still am. And you are still silent.

But I still own your mystery,
    never letting go,
    tied to you in love,
    tied to you from above,
through infinite time, through soundless space,
the spirit of your heart melting the spirit of my soul,
the holding of your hand, the falling of my tear,
until we are one again.

ONE

What if we could take a walk
          in the early evening's light,
and see shifting clouds take outline from
          the depth of a blue-rendered sky,
and hear the sound of songbirds singing
          in a world that's meant for two?

We'd be walking very slowly,
          side-by-side, our gaze upon each other,
with love felt all around us, as if in a dream,
          as if our two hearts could beat as one.
And I will be tightly holding your hands
          on the morning to be my day of

mourning—my needing to relearn as fast as I can
          all that I knew of you, of me, of us as one.
And unlearn all those things that I learned with you.
          Because now I can no longer walk
in a world that's naturally meant for two.
          Because now I am only one. ♍

If my writing seems like a lot of gibberish, that's because I have no real language for love—the language my heart speaks whenever I write to you, whenever I write a letter for us. I need to write to tell you again of my life now halved without you, hoping to build up a wall of words to reach you, hanging on to what I have written and not letting go, holding on to a dream of you, scared for dear life because a dream is all I have of you.

But you are halved also, and I hold on to you but can't see you. All I can do is pray that you are holding on to me. So that we never part. So that we are still one in spirit.

A MARVELOUS LOVE

Someone had attached a large heart-shaped piece
of cardboard to a pole on the highway not to far from
the sea-shelled beach. Speedily driving by one could
        not help
but read the phrase *I love you* neatly printed in bold red
letters within, no doubt to a very special someone.

I thought, perhaps this is a remnant from a Valentine's
Day past. Or put in place by a brash young man eager to
tell everyone in the world of his special someone. I hoped
all his effort had been seen as a perfect sign of his love.
And I wished that could have been me as a young man

in love and you the special someone in my life.
But today that is no longer our world to share.
I realized I could never have been as brash,
more likely sticking my head safely into the sand,
fearful of hearing the loving sound in your laugh.

And now, for us it is too late to do anything:
What I did do for you will never repeat,
Because efforts undone, remain undone.
Because bright red letters, weather and fade.
Because my perfect seashell, washed out to sea. ♍

Standing at the water's edge I saw breakers rolling ashore. The water was rough, the wind strong. I noticed the never-ending play of the waves: cresting and falling and crashing, flowing to shore then sliding back and rising from the ocean floor to crest again.

In no time I counted forty-five breakers, realizing how quickly forty-five years of marriage passed by. Looking through God's eyes, it must have happened in a blink. Then I noticed slow-moving and voluminous and white, billowing and soundless cumulus clouds above making their way above the frantic actions and sounds below.

I thought, there goes our life as if sculpted as part of a procession within an ancient Greek frieze, reverent as if in a solemn procession before the eyes of God. And I felt overwhelmed by your spirit.

THE LETTER THAT WASN'T

Although this is a letter, I feel it wants to be a poem,

> *with words that are soft and true,*
> *loving words reminding me of you,*

to have you still feel as special and new to me as the
newness of each morning we awoke next to each other.
You might ask me (and I can hear you speaking to me now), "But why?"
And I have an answer for you that I think you will like:

> *It's my wish to always do something more for you,*
> *more than painting your sky in a sunny hue.*

Such a work is an extension of my love, my promise
that I never forget your place in my life, and just like a
flower's replenishing seed-head, you will see in my words
a shining of spirituality, yours and mine, together, being

> *the spiritual growth that we share.*
> *It's my telling the world that I care,*
> *through a prayer, a poem, through time apart,*
> *with the words of love deep within my heart.*
> *And if my zeal should lapse (which I doubt),*
> *I want your spirit to wake me with a shout.* ♍

Today I want to write more than a letter, to reflect that this a most peaceful time of day in which I would have suggested your sitting outside in the quiet of the screened porch, at least for a short time, and hear for yourself the call of a bird lost in the thickness of a hedge. It is not an annoying sound—it sounds almost loving—because it reminds me of those times when we sat out here together, when I flew to your side to be with you, and while together in the middle of the day or the week or the month, we would hold hands.

But today how many words must be written for us to again set our eyes upon each other? I am living my years without you, waiting to break through the barrier separating us, spacing out words, and images too, to keep us together.

Today is yet another day for love, a day for writing you this letter.

WITHOUT REGARD

I thought I heard you say
my name in the silence that is today.
Regardless if its sound be lost in the heavens above,
And instead of your name is only heard the cry of a
        dove,
I will write out my prayer for you on the sand of any
        endless lot,
Even though my pen be lost or ink seeped into a cursed
        spot,
So that you may read of my love and see my arms
        raised,
In some form of oblation, some type of stilled praise,
And if in my reaching through the heavens to you,
I only touch loneliness in a sky of loving blue,
Regardless, I want to hear you clearly my name say,
Each time I write yours in the silence of every day. ♍

I read a poem today that struck me as being unique to us. And it should be because I wrote it one day when thinking of you. Writing it was hard but reading it even harder, because its words reminded me of the thoughts of love for you that flow in and out of my mind as easily as your spirit weaves in and out of my heart—the heart that knows I love you—the heart that knows I lost you.

Once in life I thought I knew everything about you that I could ever be expected to know. And once I thought I knew everything about your spirit: How I could bring you back to me, by writing with one hand and praying to God with the other. But I thought wrong and we remain separated, apart from each other, on the opposite side of the weaver's shuttle.

Once I thought I knew myself. But the only thing I do know is what is woven within my heart today.

PORTRAIT OF THE YOUNG ARTIST ON THE MORNING AFTER

The artist promised to paint the portrait of the one he held
dear to his heart tomorrow. But who knew death was
waiting when she answered the door's bell that night?
As merciless and ghastly as the snatching of life,
is the macabre tolling bell on the morning after,
when unbelief reigns among the living for their dead:
when the heart weeps for the one who is no more,
when seeking a miracle from the hand of God.
*
The night's long darkness brings to the artist
myriad memories, impossible visions of erstwhile lives:
souls of the righteous hearing heavenly harps,
those of the condemned fearing Dante's *Inferno*,
surging like a surrealistically silent wave of the sea,
blindly reaching for the loving words thought given
but now lost in a black tide of neglect to all,
probing their hearts to fathomless depths,
scrutinizing their memories in innocence,
prying tears from their eyes in guilt.
Anguished, they express sorrow but groan in seeking
release, as if unjustly and harshly imprisoned,
wailing for freedom from being no more,
flailing tinned cups across steeled bars in bloodied frenzy,
joined by hands reaching out to them from the other side.
*
On the morning after, for these souls there is no mercy,
even less pity for the artist wanting to walk in their steps,
all in unison now praying to God in unfamiliar voices.
But he saw her, the one who is no more; he called to her,
a portrait of distress groping in the shadows of dawn,

unable to be touched by him, unable to return to him.
He opened his eyes in the dawn's defining moment,
awakened by the tolling bell he most surely heard,
his body trembling, his face drawn, eyes sunken in grief,
his hand bloodied, his heart crushed,
awakening to believe in the unbelievable.
to want the impossible from God
on the morning after. ♍

When I was a young know-it-all kid, I never gave the concept of time a second thought. Time seemed infinite, a concept as hard for a kid to understand as love—as God. To me, love was only for sissies, and God only to be feared. But all that was long before I met you. When that happened, love became within my grasp to know, and after we married, God was to be respected. Our days passed still unnoticed by me because they seemed infinite.

But the day came when suddenly we were together no longer, when the time allotted to us ended, when days and nights consisted only of me. With you in my life I never noticed life, that you were my life. I begin to be aware of the passing of time, noticed first by days that going from morning to night with nothing in-between, by the quietness in a house for one that had been a home for two, and by my love for you hanging around in the corner by your bed every day and night because it had nowhere to go.

And God, no longer a concept to be only feared or respected, became the reason for my continuing love for you. But a know-it-all kid could not know that.

HERCULEAN TASKS

Beyond the saga of Greco-Roman myth,
     of man's tumultuous quest for fire,
when Mount Olympian gods parceled out to Atlas the task
     of bearing the world's weight upon his shoulders,
and to the demigod, Hercules, twelve tasks for his choice
     of Virtue in life over Pleasure,
is the modern-day saga of a heroine,
     whose hero had only one task in their lifetime,

when living upon their own Mount Olympus,
     spending their days and nights
stealthily spying upon deer crossing running Stygian
     streams in the early light of dawn;
observantly beholding fiery sunsets over mountains,
     belying the brightness of Achilles' funeral pyre;
passionately gazing upon Arcadian forests reaching all the
     way up to the heavens above;
mischievously listening to orgy-like shrieks as Pan
     seduced woodland nymphs on starry nights.

But who would have thought this god-given life would
     come with tasks too much for them to bear,
fears of traversing mountain roads in the secluded, silent,
     deep of night,
their Hades-like labors of removing on their mountain the
     snows of winter,
the mercilessly raging floods from the rains of early
     spring, extinguishing the fire of his life.

The hero became helplessly trapped within a tumultuous
     deluge from unchartered waters,
a raging of waters, a baptism freely flowing,
     past the rocky crags of their life.

The heroine lie beyond the grasp of her hero's hand,
      tragically drowned among the firmly planted
memory vines of his mind, unable to pray for what was
      never to be decreed for them by God.

In his soulful quest for heaven on earth, how the broken
      hero desired to again hold her close to his heart,
to calm her fears and hold her hands,
      to give the tenderness he now will only write of.
And if her hero has difficulty in beginning these pages,
      in bearing the weight of his world upon his lonely
shoulders, it is all part of his Herculean task,
      to say his words to her. ♍

FREEFORM

There is so much time
I want to spend with you but can't,
so much I want to say but don't know how,
so much gentleness I want to freely give you
but must stop muted, stalled, dead in my tracks.
Perhaps in sleep a dream of you will freely form
and materialize, and a kiss between us exchanged,
a glance realized, a touch once again lovingly felt.
But my sleep will be the brother of your death,
and my grief is the sister of all our sorrows,
and those of which I will no longer hide:
how to tell you in words you can hear,
how I may give you my love for
ever, how to exist without
you in my arms, now
all the things I
need you
to know
forever.
♍

INCOMPLETE

Finding yourself now alone and living in strife,
is like losing what makes up the completeness of life.
It's like reading the last letter from one you still love
in silence with thoughts now lost in heaven above.

The police want a picture of what you have lost,
but no matter the number of lines that you draw,
there is no new creation that can give them more.

It's as if searching for someone you no longer see,
a vision familiar—not vague—in your memory,
and needing to be remembered eternally.

And what of creations not done, lying untended,
or of the life unfinished and which now has ended?
Must life be as undone, as incomplete as this?
No, for today you are lost in God's completeness. ♍

KNOWING

I was hoping that it was you calling
when I heard the telephone ring today.
It's been a long while since I've been treated to the
sound of your voice, or give you the sound of mine.
But you know all that.

However, if your call is not
forthcoming, I can always read
you this poem, because it contains
the same words of love I would have
preferred to be able to say to you in person,
words I said the last time my own eyes saw you,
in the winter, the coldest winter and deadliest of our life.
I always know that.

However, any season is a lonely time being without you,
all because you are so far from home and from me.
And I'll always know all that.

You would be here with me if you could.
But you know that, too. ♍

AN ODE TO THE ONLY WOMAN HE'LL ALWAYS LOVE

It started out being a morning just like any other at the hospital, even if he was late to welcome newly admitted patients for the Chaplin. Entering his office he quickly learned that someone had left the radio playing all night. And he became annoyed because he couldn't care less for the sound of pop music—although if he did hear or felt something that for some reason struck him deeply, he became attached to it. As it was the time he met the girl fifty years ago who would become his wife. As it was each time he volunteered at the hospital.

He was embarrassed to admit he was late because of oversleeping. Instead, he paid attention to the radio announcer saying that the next song would be what he called an ode for his male listeners, to celebrate the only woman they've ever loved on this one particular day, Valentine's Day.

But there was little time to listen because of a long list of patients to visit, and before beginning to make his rounds to the various floors he was handed a note requesting prayers for a particular patient on the third floor. Without paying attention, he merely tucked the paper behind his list and began. When he thought himself finished, he came across that added request. Making his way again through the busy hospital corridors, hearing once again the lullaby always heard to inform of a new life born in the nursery, he arrived at the patient's door, knocked and walked in, anticipating his day's completion.

The patient, a frail-looking elderly white-haired woman was alone and sitting up in her darkened room. He wondered why this patient would not want her room brighter, but all he knew was her name: Anna.

Her eyes appeared tired, her face forlorn. In response to his greeting, she slowly turned them, simply extending her hand as he offered her a rote sheet of prayers, explaining these are standard prayers offered to all hospital patients to read. But she softly said, "I'm blind. And I'm Jewish."

Startled by her response, his fingers fumbled to find a reading that would acknowledge her presence. He was looking for a eureka moment, like a symbolic light bulb flashing over his head upon his discovery of an appropriate prayer, hoping that she would be blind also to his feeling of uneasiness.

He remembered the time of fearing in dread,
* When his wife was the ill one lying in bed,*
When he cared so much more about only being next to her,
* If he prayed for themselves it was silently done, only a*
* blur.*

He became startled again when at the sound of his voice she decidedly extended her hand to him, as if in need to hold onto something for dear life, fearing to let go. He was familiar with that feeling and held her hand.

This was his first time to hold a woman's hand,
* Since that time of the only one in all of his land,*
And imagining himself to be holding a magician's black
* cape,*
* The quick sweep of which would have them together*
* escape.*

He left this patient's room with the uncomfortable feeling that he had cheated her from something she needed, promising himself to return to her the next day, picturing his search for a prayer for this patient named Anna. It would be more meaningful to her, even if he had to search all night.

But when returning to her room the next day and finding it unoccupied, he asked the entering nurse about the patient who was there yesterday. She replied in a matter-of-fact voice, "Oh, she died during the night." Anna left his life before he could give her the sound of a prayer that came from his heart. And he uncomfortably felt the way he felt when the music that made up his life died. Feeling cheated from the chance to offer her spiritual reassurance, he said lamely he hoped at least that the people who loved her were at her side.

> *Man is unprepared for life to end,*
> *To leave his love, his only best friend,*
> *When hands are not released when two hearts are stilled,*
> *When one is yet to die but the other is already killed,*

And then came his eureka moment like a crescendo falling upon him. The crushing sound opened his eyes when he realized that the third floor hospital room in which he had prayed only the day before lie directly across from the room in which he had grasped onto his wife's hand for the last time not too long ago. But he never really let go of her hand and today quietly sings the words of a lullaby to her, sometimes even more than one, staying awake each and every night.

> *And so my ode is now over,*
> *Also is your life and mine as a lover,*
> *But I'm still your spouse; my words fly to God like a dove,*
> *The words I give to the only woman I will always love.* ♍

THE FRAGRANCE OF A ROSE

That pink rose I bought
(You know the one I mean),
Has opened wide two petals,
Poised as if in a dream,

As if ready to take flight,
But I know it never will,
It holds the key to my heart
and will not leave still

waiting for you to swoop down
upon me smiling at a rose.
The fragrance of your greeting
is the sweetness of its pose. ♍

There is a feeling of love in the air tonight that I cannot ignore. It causes me to want to sit beside you, to hold your hand, to kiss your face, to look into your eyes, to see your smile, to softly say I love you—only that phrase. Because I am at a loss for words; because my eyes see the rose in our bedroom with all the color and majesty and splendor from when I placed it there; because I sense your closeness and am unwilling to break the spirituality of this moment with the sound of my voice. If my words could paint your portrait as I see you know, I would have a classical masterpiece—a work of substance and beauty—an indication of what my spiritual heart looks like. And I can release you and drift off to sleep now that you are comfortably next to me and within my grasp, thanking God for his gifts of love and you. This is our love; this is all I need.

MORTALLY MORIBUND

Walking out from the ashes of the Bitter Valley,
   a wounded mourning dove searches for his mate,
   his wings bear non-healing scars, incurable wounds,
but still hold a promise of life, of spring, of renewal.

Winter's violence caused no lack of sorrows for the two,
      one lying on a bed of death,
      the other stepping silently toward her side,
seeking a miracle, finding none, failing, loving to the end.

The living have been diminished through God's will,
      each in their own way, the winter dying to spring,
      and water coursing again, melting bared hearts,
bonds as ever-flowing as the sea, until eternity.

Wounded lovers long to heal,
      to relive the first moments known to each other,
      to recall the last moments of the very last breath of
life, journeying from the Valley beneath God's wings. ♍

*After so much suffering on earth, life can't just end
or we would no better than the beasts of the forest to
be destroyed, without souls, without endlessly beating
hearts.*

AFFINITY

To you I ask, what is this thing called affinity?
Should it be confused with infinity?
Some may think it's a pompous word,
others perhaps even something to avoid.
Wiser ones venture not even one guess,
Consulting first a dictionary's wordage.
But you would tell me what you think,
Even though no one cares to sink

to the depths of silent ramblings,
of loss of life, of why a heart no longer sings
For affinity to you is a parallel of sameness
with another, with no need to second-guess
not for any outward appearance,
but for what is unseen: perseverance
And so it was when you met whom you loved;
It was like being you, yourself, not being shoved

Or set aside in a corner and left all alone,
With nary a word to share or condone.
With kindness and friendship all through the day,
A mingling of spirits through the entire fray
Of death and separation in a battle askew,
As if I am still living, as if married anew.
Proving to all you are my affinity,
And why I'll love you to infinity. ♍

ELEGAIC REMEMBRANCE 1
Seek First The Kingdom Of God

Together they searched for wisdom and understanding:
a man, weak and short-lived,
a woman, fragile but who no longer lived,
each unknowing the wisdom of God's distance and time.

In the length of their measured time on earth,
their spiritual distance seems to shorten
whenever he hears her funerary hymn.
So that he is aware of closeness to her,
of being transported back in time with her,
to still be dependent upon her being there for him;
                        and recalling
when they kept their soul private and their prayer silent,
in their early days, now seemingly carefree,
but marred by life's uncertainties and problems,
now exposed like demolished facade of a home,
revealing for the first time its once inner private soul
for the world to see, for God to judge;
                        and remembering
the first time she surprised him by standing at the top of
the stairs to greet him at day's end,
when suddenly their kitchen was all aglow with her
surefire movements of slicing and cutting and chopping
into sundry bowls and dishes and wok,
smiling in her creation of her first oriental dinner;
                        and wincing

at the piled of utensils towered up for cleaning,
blinded to the look of happiness in her eyes,
blindly holding back his silent love for her,
blind to everything, especially his tower of Babel;
                    and revealing
the day their life became tragic,
when he failed to see God's footprints in their life,
when her eyes closed for the last time,
when she could not see his tower crashing over him,
or the now-exposed silenced love within his heart,
his prayerful kneeling,
when life's broken thread unraveled,
when he believed God had abandoned them.

Blindly reaching out through measured distance,
where shall their two spirits meet?
God will judge the love felt within the human heart
having yet to learn of spiritual distance and time. ♍

*I may be wrong but I don't think anything can compare
with receiving a surprise—especially when anticipating
one, like the surprise of receiving a new and unexpected
rose added to all those which have been already given
you. And even if you are aware of receiving one, there's
always something new and exciting about seeing it for the
first time with your own eyes.*

*The anticipation of a loving encounter is like that.
And I love giving you that anticipation with my words,
through time and distance, through life and into death.
But if you discover that the words I have used are few,
look into my heart, deeply, to discover those still waiting
to be born on paper for you and waiting to surprise you.*

ELEGAIC REMEMBRANCE 2
The Gardener's Final Visit

My Letter of Farewell:

Your white roses are trimmed for the very last time.
      They will need cutting no longer.
You won't be needing my help and now I will be alone.
      But then, so are you…
And I think of how one rose could foretell life.
      But yet, so it does.

You have always been a part of their days, their nights,
      of their white displays,
Their filling the emptiness of a vase with soft richness,
      petals only to fade… to fall…
To complete their days of glory, somberly and silently
      removed, no longer in sight…

…and placed before the altar of God,
      as also on this day are you.
not ready to live a life of only one…
      but yet so you are, so am I,
your Gardener in life. ♍

ELEGIAC RESIGNATION 3
Generational Gap

You would think it easy to re-assemble a shattered life,
  one broken in half and now incomplete.
The voices of life in chorus say, "Simply pick up the
  pieces and begin anew."
But wouldn't that be bringing life to a generation of the
  young touting to know all about the old?
Or intruding upon an older generation of wisdom, one
  purporting to know better than the young?

Whatever your generation, you had no choice but to
  watch life fall from your hands,
shattering into long shards, like a pane of glass with
  penetratingly sharp edges producing
sharp stabbings of loneliness, painful punctures of futility,
  the hole in life known to every generation,
to give and receive love, to remember what once was and
  fearfully soon forgot.

So that in anger for not knowing where to stand,
  with one hand a shard is picked up to hurl back at life,
and to those who do not understand this now is your life,
  with the other writing of a remembered side of your life.
And what could be worse than forging ahead with a gang
  but leaving former days of completeness forgotten?
For your remembered side will always be half of your
  generation. ♍

ELEGIAC RESIGNATION 4
City Dump

What can be said of a city dump?
After all…
        …what does one really see?
Acres of land but no place to sit, to gaze upon a lonely
        tree,
perhaps with broken remnants of a solid foundation of
        yore,
and what was once a lovely home, now only a closed
        door,
the ghost of its gingerbread cornice, an eerie and cold
        sight,
is lost to the drabness of day and hidden in the dead of
        night,
where real people once lived and died,
but now there is no place to hide.

With a rock thrown here and a path leading nowhere,
lost in grief that leaves one disarrayed and with a tortuous
        stare,
life will put you in a dump at times of squalor and strife,
a far cry from what was once the luxury of a tranquil life,
feeling like the blade of grass caught in a vise-like
        cracked brick,
in rain or in sun its life is stilled, swept away with a flick.

One may search far and wide in heaven's ever-distant
        light,
to ask God for wisdom to see what is beyond the night,
to know there's more to life that eye can see or mind can
        store
of a husband and wife today lost to each other
        forevermore,
in that part of a city, of which it is always to be thought,
to run from and hide, for there is nothing which can be
        sought.

Between the lands of sunrise and sunset exist no sounds
        of laughter or mirth,
for a dump's damaged brick needing reuse and rebirth. ♍

There is no one but you I want to share life with, or whatever is the opposite of life found at the end of a long dark tunnel. What seems to be a light at its end is a door to my mind kept closed and locked, fearful of its opening, finding you swept away from me, finding myself alone.

I was alone on the day before the foundation of our wedding was built.

On that day I married you for life and what for lies beyond, so that we can discover what lies beyond that closed door together.

MIND, HEART, AND MUTUAL COLLEAGUE

With confidence in a natural world and a methodical mind to solve the most baffling of problems, he would sit back and smile peacefully as he sits back with hands clasped together and placed behind his head in his private world. And with stirring passion, he could faultlessly write any hypothesis to any colleague who would ask him. However, don't ask him to compose a letter to his own wife. Then, he would find himself blocked and vexed because he was unable to logically proceed. But on one particular day, after putting aside that task for far too long, he intuitively felt its need.

But he never realized how much his logical brain and emotional heart would need nimble hands for composing the simplest of letters, for him to be as accomplished a master wordsmith as he could ever be—the way an author needs a reader—the way a husband needs his wife. He wanted words that would faultlessly fly onto paper and his hand to keep pace with his thoughts needing to be told. After all, didn't his heart know what he wanted to say?

But the actual words his heart lovingly understood were difficult for his brain to clearly comprehend. And patiently waiting and poised was his hand, sitting upon a blank sheet of paper, wanting to be told of the words to explain his where, why, and how to her. When that happened, everything was in a stalemate between logic and emotion, a deadlock when his mind shut down and mental and physical paralysis began. And his heart wept in realizing that it, too, was stalemated, but had so much to say. Confounded by the situation, he began to panic. But he closed his eyes, took a deep breath and began to think only of his wife; of the love within his heart; of how he would begin to write as much as he can to her; of not wanting to even think about his not being near her.

And then he fast-forwarded his thinking and recalled the unnatural conditions causing his wife to no longer be with him; that he is alone in everything; that writing is all he can do, rocking his mind like a shot heard around his world, jolting his brain into receiving the loving words from his heart then transmitted to his hand, and the page he is writing begins to faultlessly fill with the words of love he needed to write.

In the end, his page is filled with words, his hand is tired from writing all the sentiments of his heart, his brain befriends mindful thoughts to be prayerfully kept, her spirit joins his heart, as he sits back with hands clasped together and placed behind his head, at peace in his world. ♍

ELEGAIC RESIGNATION 5
Control

While your hand is held fast in mine,
and my gaze is fixed upon your face,
to control life for us is my goal.
But I fear life is winning the race.
     For I cannot quell a raging sea
     or save a sinking ship from devastation,
Nor hide my halting shadowed words of love,
my thoughts of an impending conflagration,

In happier times of placid peace
No thought is given to their ending;
In hapless times filled with raging anger
no thought is given to their mending.
     But now there is no time for regrets.
     Now we have but these moments,
in the deafening roars that I hear,
of clashing seas and rain in torrents.

Holding tightly as onto a broken rudder,
fearing my first real day without each other,
I want my love to be in control of our life, to not end.
And in the war between God's will and mine, I will bend.
     Which is stronger when wed, when two become
         one?
     Which is more feared when dead, when life is
         done?
Now your hand is released. My gaze descends.
Shadows will now control my life until it ends. ♍

In addition to this letter, I need to give you something else for me to feel I am in control of its words, to feel they are complete. But whatever it is, I know of its value to my heart, and like my heart it is one of a kind. So that for now, I give what I have to your spirit, which will not mind if the petals of a rose are no longer young, or if the words I write are old, because their symbolic meanings are always new.

But even if I should discover there is nothing additional to give you today, I close this letter by saying I love you. And this solitary phrase makes your letter complete to me—as complete as two lovers with their eyes locked in an embrace on a starry night.

ELEGAIC RESIGNATION 6
A Litany of Circumstance

My wish for all is to have a happy new year,
    To exclaim it loudly for the all world to hear,
for everyone in good faith to boldly receive,
    Even those souls who today still loudly grieve.
How slight when my wish is nothing more than a phrase,
    Never paying tribute to mark an end of days.
How empty when each new day becomes so very long,
    When I questioned: Now, just where do I belong?

Futile are attempts to pray to God with silenced hearts,
    To pray a litany with an end that never starts,
And to say I lived to give all my love to you forevermore,
    And my hand to keep in yours forever as we soar,
And my heart to touch, to know that my love pours,
    And my every fallen tear to now be wed to yours,
And my wretchedness in now living without your glance,
    And those times we looked at each other askance,

On this day of newness today not existing for me,
    Or you, on this day of silence within my litany. ♍

Never wanting to end this or any year without ever giving you something of myself, I am writing this letter, which some say you will never know of. But they don't understand that I will read it for you.

I tried to read and reread your mind when I heard what was to become your very last word to me. But that was an impossible task because your word was open-ended, incomplete, and an ending in itself. It stood as an end to our forty-five years of marriage as we appeared before each other from the edges of life and death. In hearing, I heard our finality; I heard your helplessness. And then, complete silence followed.

I write to you in my silence today. And I hope you can hear me say I always need to feel close to you. Because I have an image of you smiling and want to see your smile again. Because I want to say a litany of God-inspired love.

ELEGAIC RESIGNATION 7
The Mysterious Mountain

Lost in a cloudy haze of mystery looms a mountain,
  Below the vault of heaven above,
  obscured in the mist below.
  Veiled in secrecy, as nonexistent as God,
  perhaps it is.

But the mountain is as real to a lone wayfarer
  as is his dream not forgotten,
  his vision of what was, drawing forward,
  walking faster and faster, so as to not be lost yet again.

His stride matters not; the mountain never comes closer,
  nor does his vision; his image of her fades away,
  and with it their only chance to leap across life's
  mountains, together in spirit,
  hand in hand.

Despite its majesty, a mountain has no vision,
  no wisdom, no knowledge of love,
  nor of the touch of a hand as soft as God's.
  Its stormy winds push forward;
  its rocky slopes pull back.

Engulfed, the wayfarer cannot turn back,
  but he also cannot move forward
  through the earthquake of a solitary life
  or pass a mountain of eternal truth
  speaking to him:

No one can bargain with the will of God.
    A mysterious mountain in his path
    is his own creation.
    For the wisdom of God
    will always move mountains. ♍

I looked for you today
but couldn't find you.
I suddenly felt very small
and lonely without you.
But the rose in our bedroom
appears to be living forever.
So that I know you are near.
And I also know that a rose is
as spiritual as a husband seeking his wife
but who cannot see beyond the
mountain before him

ELEGAIC RESIGNATION 8
Unfinished Business

"Fire! My house is on fire!"
Frantically, I can barely get the words out to the 9-1-1 operator.
"Get everyone out. Evacuate now!" is the stark command, the
tone of his voice demanding action.
I hurriedly begin to leave. But in my confusion I remember
a most important business trip tomorrow that must be cancelled
thinking about the first call I should make, rushing past the table at
the living room window – an altar table, the store merchant called
it—and its symbolic quilted covering.
Both had been recently purchased to cheer my wife upon her
hospital release and return home, leading me to recall the grave
condition her doctors told me of. But I refused to believe. And so
I was too late when I rushed to the hospital at the last minute. For
me to have the chance to place one last kiss upon her lips. For her to
hear me say for the last time, I love you.

□

Outside, I immediately become aware of firefighters and
onlookers justifiably concerned about flames reaching their nearby
homes in the suburban development. Suddenly I cry out, "The
quilt!" now regretting I left behind the stitched coverlet on the table.
It was to be my fitting remembrance of her, I did not want it to be
also destroyed.
Rushing to the still closed front door, people are shouting at me
not to enter, but I turn the now hot-to-the-touch doorknob. With an
unexplainable inner surge of strength felt in my arms, the door comes

free of its hinges. I fling it up in the night air as if its construction was only of stiffened cardboard and enter the flaming interior.

Closing my eyes to eerily dancing shadows of flames upon the walls, I could still hear their ominous crackling and feel their heat. I rush through the smoky haze to the altar table.

Suddenly, before me I see my wife already standing in front of the bare table, holding the now neatly folded quilt in her arms. With the look of love in her eyes I thought I would never see again, I am given a kiss as she hands me the quilt. I feel my eyes beginning to tear.

"I love you," I want to cry out to her above the crackling sound of the flames around us, needing to hear myself speak the words that were never said between us. But I can only mouth them because they are stuck in my throat, exactly as I know they would have been in a hospital room.

I race outside unharmed by the fire, holding tightly to the quilt. With people quickly surrounding me, someone in the crowd touches it and quickly bolts back, asking me, "How can you hold that? It's as hot as fire." "You must be dreaming," I knowingly reply.

Firemen gather around to make sure I have not been burned, admonishing me for going into the fire. I hear one disparagingly remark to another, "The fool." All I can do is nostalgically say, "She kissed me."

☐

The next day in somber silence I enter my house.

In the living room, everything is gone, destroyed amid still-smoking embers, including the special table. The white carpeting is completely charred - except for two sets of footprints set toe to toe, which have remained white where the quilt had been.

Upon awakening, I feel tears are in my eyes. ♍

At times I don't know what to say, what to share.
Perhaps the spirit of this biblical verse from Song of
Solomon says it for me:

> *Set me as a seal on your heart,*
> *As a seal on your arm,*
> *For love is as strong as death,*
> *Passion as fierce as the grave,*
> *Its flashes are flames of fire,*
> *A blazing flame.*

My letters to you
are expressions of
love and commitment.
But I cannot live them with you,
 only write to you of my love, devotion,
fear sorrow, guilt, suffering, and anxiety.
These feelings document what we
could not share with each other at our end.
They speak of our beginning and our goodbye.
They are symbols of our unique closure.
They are the flames of our blazing fire.

SIXTY-THREE MINUTES

Even if he had all the time in the world, even if he wasn't irked by the prolonged wait in the florist shop, the reserved statistician would still impatiently exclaim in a frustrated show of emotion, "Will this line ever move?" He expected to hear a reaction from among the throng of last minute shoppers lined up on Valentine's Day.

"Wait your turn like everyone else, old codger," derided one. Another snickered. A third complacently laughed.

Tenderhearted barbarians, he thought.

Angry but not violent, austere though hopelessly sentimental, he was used to their reaction, remembering supermarket aisles jammed with shopping carts and shoppers turned into gossipers holding him back and mindlessly chattering away while he helplessly felt like their prisoner. And today he was even less tolerant of all those all clamoring to buy roses for their special some ones, belying his belief that Valentine's Day was only a day like any other.

However that could never be for him because of his long ingrained belief, an innate animal instinct, to bring his wife roses with every annual passage of this day, a ritual he had faithfully observed for more years than he wished to remember.

The pressing crowd became annoying. He was in a hurry to move on, to finish shopping, to return home. There was too much to remember, he bristled, and no time to forget. But upon his arrival at the front counter, the sales clerk promptly informed him that they were sold out of red roses and instead pointed to what was available, anxious to handpick something for him. Frustrated, he dashed from the shop in a huff carrying only a single subdued-in-color red-violet rose unaccompanied by neither a pre-printed add-on message nor holiday greeting card. It was as if both husband and wife had become nameless to the outside world.

□

Nearly fifty Valentine's Days' past he had looked deeply into the eyes of the young woman who would soon become his wife and blushingly gave her a heart-shaped box of chocolates and bouquet of bright red roses. After all, they had been engaged for three months and would be married in nine more. And he liked to think of themselves on that first Valentine's Day as being swept free from troubles, devoid of uncertainties and heartaches, away from worldly concerns. It was a time reserved only for them, a time to be young forever, and with his uncanny devotion to numbers, to live that numberless array of days together.

Upon arriving home, his immediate concern was where to place the lone bloom. He promptly dismissed the dining room, feeling that even a scant burst of color there would not be appropriate, remembering the image of his smiling wife taking from him whatever flower he brought her. Then, he would blithely step into the background silently studying the sparkle in her eyes as she bustled about making that room the final destination for any bright bouquet he gave her. But that was before she became ill. And after illness took its final toll, he stepped back again, this time to somberly feel that her funeral was his also.

Months later, he would bitterly grieve to the priest who had married them that he was angry with himself because couldn't even lay claim to having a dream of his wife, logically reasoning that, after all, a dream would be the only way he could ever see her again. Whatever slight smile he might have borne would quickly turn into a scowl accompanied with furrowed brows and pursed lips as he began again to feel the pain of his wife's leaving that he paradoxically never wanted to forget, now that he lived only for himself.

Walking upstairs irate with himself because of his inability to make a simple decision about a flower, he narrowed his choice of location to the bedroom, realistically reasoning that roses are only here one day and gone the next, unlike numbers which last forever. He set the narrow glass vase on the bedside night table with the lone digital clock adjacent to his wife's side of the bed. It seemed strange to him how the color from only one flower could fill that corner of the room with life, nostalgically sensing it could never be too early or ever be too late for him to wish for her the gladness felt by many on this day, sadly remembering that this will be the first year he would not be presented with a smile from his wife.

□

The stilled shadows of dusk became the sullen solitude of night. From the bedroom window he peered upward at the glittering stars looking like an array of stilled souls not wanting for anything against their backdrop of black velvet space.

Settling into bed he took one last look at his clock before putting the room into darkness and gradually drifting into sleep. But in the middle of a restless night he awoke and glanced at the clock whose red numerals announced that the time was 11:17pm. Then, he closed his eyes once again, this time with his hands clasped as if in prayerful repose.

Then, in the brightness of another day, he was entering a building to give his wife a surprise birthday present. Inside, there in silence stood a vision of her. His dream-filled eyes saw her standing helplessly behind the barred door of a jail cell, looking at him with mournful eyes. Walking to the cell door, he opened it and entered. She stepped back and sat down keeping her gaze upon him. He felt the sadness in her unsmiling expression. In silence, their eyes met. In silence, he stood before her and bent down to kiss her. Ever so close, their lips nearly touching, the vision silently and rapidly evaporated.

He awoke with a start, finding himself staring at the numbers of the clock on the other side of the bed. Its red phosphorescent display glowed onto the adjacent vase holding the rose, which he could not see in the darkness. But he knew it was there and that an hour had passed because the time now was 12:20am, although it seemed to him as if only a second of time had passed.

In the darkness, in a bright flash of instant recognition, he put together those two seemingly disparate sets of numbers that he had only read as time, this time seeing two dates: that of their wedding to each other, and that of their parting from each other—nothing less than the lifetime of years accumulated past that first Valentine's Day they spent together. Only now his measures of time became his metrics of love for his wife, spanning from the darkness of one night into the future light of yet a new day, with husband and wife together in spirit and unfettered by time, nothing less than a non-perishable Valentine's Day rose shared between them, not picked by hand and lasting forever.

Remaining in darkness but throwing off the stupor of sleep he slowly sat up and remembered his dream, aware of the lone tear now slowly descending his face, aware that all the frustrations of his life counted for nothing. Even if he returned to sleep and never woke again, even if his soul rose up to heaven, because of sixty-three minutes, he had finally received what he needed and always wanted. ♍

SEPTUAGENARIAN

Many years ago,
When I was twenty-four,
It was a very good year
          for meeting a girl and changing both our lives.
I looked into her eyes,
A chance meeting—nothing more,
That day I turned twenty-four.

The very next year,
My life would have been full,
But for the very sad year
          for losing that girl, the one love of my life.
Now she lives within my heart,
The heart no longer alive,
When our years were forty-five.

Now my days are done,
And my nighttime descends.
Now all alone once again,
          I live the heartfelt thoughts that made up our life:
How it all started from naught,
Growing through smiles and tears,
Ours have been very good years. ♍

Instead of a birthday gift, which you would have put into one of your colorful gift bags, you have given me the gift of your spirit. So that it doesn't matter if we are separated today, on my birthday, the day we met. We are joined as one in spirit. We cannot be separated, because I cannot separate myself from you. My words are not separated from my emotions—feelings—love for you. I want to sound like a broken record, because we are broken in life, but not in spirit.

Through the grace of God, our one spirit is stronger than our two individual lives—the way that the holy spirit of God is stronger than all the "evil ones" in the world—the way my love for you is stronger than I am.

IN CONCLUSION

Truly,
only the
lonely-hearted
can understand
the desire
to bypass life,
to turn poet,
to write phrases
as metaphors
of portraiture
dedicated to
his inspiration,
his subject,
his wife...

*...and I picture you now, reading one of my early letters,
written with my closed eyes, reflecting upon our hopes in
life, our times to be, the love felt within my heart...*

...leaving
me to ponder
the imponderable,
until the day I finally reach
the final ending of all my days,
until we are as close to each other,
as close as a pen is to a sheet of paper,
and I see you with the
opened eyes of my heart.

For my love endures forever. ♍

Give thanks to the Lord,
for he is good;
for his love endures forever.

Psalm 118

www.ingramcontent.com/pod-product-compliance
Lightning Source LLC
Chambersburg PA
CBHW030756150426
42813CB00068B/3174/J

9781466905306